T
Beml
Bran

Peter A. Harding

O2 class 0-4-4T No.W.14 "Fishbourne" arriving at Brading Station with the branch train from Bembridge. July 4th 1953.   R.F.Roberts

Published by

Peter A. Harding

"Mossgiel", Bagshot Road, Knaphill,
Woking, Surrey GU21 2SG.

ISBN 0 9552403 0 1

First published 1988. Revised edition 2006.
© Peter A. Harding 2006.
*Printed by Binfield Print & Design Ltd.,
Binfield Road, Byfleet Village, Surrey KT14 7PN.*

Contents

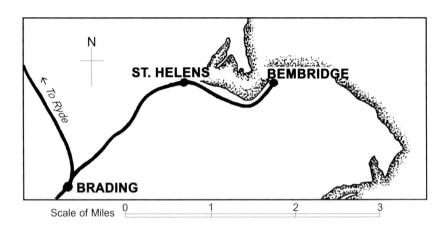

N

← To Ryde

ST. HELENS   BEMBRIDGE

BRADING

Scale of Miles   0   1   2   3

O2 class 0-4-4T No.W.14 "Fishbourne" waits at Bembridge Station, ready to return to Brading with the branch train. May 23rd 1953.   R.F.Roberts

Introduction

The Bembridge branch line was opened to passengers in May 1882 after a vast land reclaim scheme on the Isle of Wight had been carried out by the Brading Harbour Improvement & Railway Company, who had hoped to develop St. Helens into a major port and transform Bembridge into a popular seaside resort.

In August 1886, a train-ferry service started between Langston* Harbour on the Hayling Island branch line and St. Helens but, unfortunately, this service was discontinued in March 1888.

Although the port at St. Helens remained very busy for many years, trade gradually declined in favour of the Medina Wharf which was rebuilt by the Southern Railway in the late 1920's.

Bembridge retained its charm and seclusion but never really developed into the popular seaside resort that the speculators had hoped for and the friendly little branch line became just a leisurely byway for just a few passengers.

On September 20th 1953, the branch was finally closed but, like so many other similar branch lines which disappeared during the 1950's and 1960's, it is still held in much affection by older local people and rural railway enthusiasts alike.

*Although spelt "Langstone", the London, Brighton & South Coast Railway who had operated the Hayling Island branch since 1871 decided in 1873 to drop the 'e' from the station name, although the area continued to be called Langstone as it does to this day.

Terrier 0-6-0T No.W.11 "Newport" approaching the branch bay platform at Brading Station with the train from Bembridge. July 23rd 1935.   S.W.Baker

3

History of the Line

After various proposals, the first railway line to be built on the Isle of Wight was the Cowes & Newport Railway which gained Parliamentary sanction on August 8th 1859 and was opened on June 16th 1862.

The second line on the Island was a more ambitious project built by the Isle of Wight Railway who were incorporated as the Isle of Wight (Eastern Section) Railway on July 23rd 1860 to construct a line from Ryde to Ventnor.

Construction was under the supervision of Sir John Fowler and the first section from Ryde (later called Ryde St. Johns Road) to Shanklin via Brading and Sandown was opened on August 23rd 1864 but, due to unforeseen delays the Sandown to Ventnor section was not opened until September 10th 1866 after the excavation of deep cuttings and construction of a tunnel under St. Boniface Down were carried out.

By this time the company had dropped the "Eastern Section" from their title after powers had been obtained in 1863 for a branch to Newport, although this branch was never built.

While the Ryde to Shanklin section was being constructed, both St. Helens and Bembridge on the very eastern side of the Island figured in proposals for a branch to run from this new line. First in 1863 for a line from Rowborough (north of Brading) via St. Helens and over the causeway to Bembridge and then the following year a scheme known as the Bembridge Railway, to run from a junction at Yarbridge (south of Brading) along the south side of Brading Harbour to Bembridge.

Both these schemes failed to materialise but, a short branch (more a spur) from the new station at Brading was opened to serve the quays at Brading Harbour.

At this time Brading was a fishing village and stood on the estuary of the River Yar which formed a vast natural inland harbour and was reached from the sea through a narrow mouth between St. Helens and Bembridge.

Brading Harbour before it was reclaimed. The short branch leading to the quays can just be made out to the right of the centre of the photograph. Author's Collection

Brading Harbour had a long history. In the middle ages there was the Port of Brading which was strengthened by King Edward I as a defence against French raids.

Later in 1620, Sir Hugh Myddleton tried to reclaim the land which formed the seabed at Brading Harbour by building an embankment from St. Helens to Bembridge. By 1622 work was completed but, by 1630 the embankment had burst and the whole project was abandoned.

Two hundred and forty four years later, a second scheme involving Brading Harbour was proposed by the Brading Harbour Improvement & Railway Company which was financed by the Liberator Building Society Group and received the Brading Harbour Improvement & Railway Act in 1874. The object of this Act was not only to reclaim the land which formed the seabed of Brading Harbour by building an embankment between St. Helens and Bembridge but, also to extend the railway from the quay at Brading to a new quay at St. Helens and then on to Bembridge where the company was also to build a hotel near to their new station.

The Liberator Building Society had been formed in London by Jabez Spencer Balfour in June 1868 and had grown at such a rate that it far outstripped anything that the building society world had experienced at the time. In developing Whitehall Court in London, they pioneered the fashionable flat system. Other London developments included the Cecil and Victoria Hotels as well as further flats in the Albert and Carlyle Mansions.

Work on the new embankment between St. Helens and Bembridge started almost immediately with thousands of tons of rubble, chalk and clay (brought from Bembridge Down and Portsdown Hill near Portsmouth) dumped into the sea to form a barrier to exclude the sea from Brading Harbour. Sluices were to be provided to control the outlet of the River Yar.

The engineer appointed by the Brading Harbour Improvement & Railway Company was R. J. H. Saunders who had previously been engaged on the construction of the Isle of Wight (Newport Junction) Railway from Newport to Sandown.

The contractors were Scott & Edwards of Melmerby, Yorkshire who used for the construction of the first part of the line to St. Helens, a 2-4-0 well tank which they called "St. Helens". In March 1875, while Scott & Edwards were also constructing the Alcester to Bearley line for the Great Western Railway, they had a Manning Wardle 0-6-0 saddle tank delivered new to Stratford-on-Avon where they named it "Stanley". When this locomotive was transferred to the Island in March 1879 to complete the Bembridge contract, it was perhaps not surprisingly renamed "Bembridge".

On completion of their work, both locomotives "St. Helens" and "Bembridge" were sold to the Brading Harbour Improvement & Railway Company.

In March 1877, while construction was taking place, the St. Helens Oyster Fishery Company was awarded £8,000 compensation from the Brading Harbour Improvement & Railway Company, after taking legal action concerning loss of property.

In anticipation of the forthcoming passenger service, station buildings at St. Helens and Bembridge were built in 1877, three years before the completion of the embankment and five years before the line was opened for passengers, although goods traffic was worked as far as St. Helens Quay from August 1878.

In February 1880 the barrier was finally closed but was soon breached by the sea at a point near Bembridge. This breach was filled in at a cost of over £10,000, bringing the total expenditure to a reported £420,000.

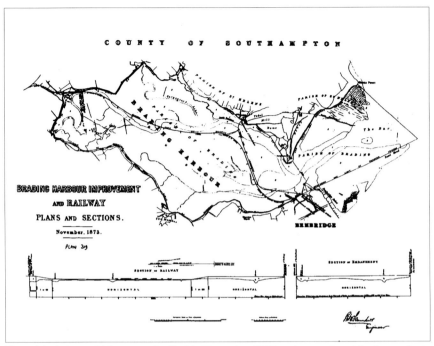

The original plans which were submitted in November 1873 and were signed by the engineer R.J.H.Saunders.

When the new embankment was considered safe, a roadway was built along the top. This road was to become a toll road owned by the Company.

The whole 2³/₄ mile branch line from Brading to Bembridge was finally opened for passengers on Saturday, May 27th, 1882 and the *Isle of Wight Times* of Thursday, June 1st, 1882 covered the event with the following two paragraphs in their Brading Section:-

BRADING Harbour's new railway is in a fair state of completion. The line was inspected on Wednesday last by Colonel Yolland R.E., Her Majesty's Inspector of Railways and found to be in a sufficiently satisfactory condition to warrant his passing the line for passenger traffic. On Saturday, passengers were conveyed over the line for the first time.

At Brading a suitable station has been erected, platform widened, a new siding constructed and a handsome signal station adorns the eastern embankment. Arrangements have been made for working the new line of railway which will be under the management of Mr. J. Bourne.

The *Isle of Wight Observer* briefly stated:-

The engine which drew the opening train was decorated with flowers. . . and about three hundred of the villagers of St. Helens and Bembridge were brought into Ryde for nothing.

The Royal Spithead Hotel at Bembridge, which was also owned by the Brading Harbour Improvement & Railway Company was opened on July 15th, 1882. A party consisting of the company chairman, Jabez Spencer Balfour (who had by now become one of Tamworth's two Liberal M.P.'s), the directors and other interested personnel travelled down from London to Portsmouth where they sailed direct to Bembridge by the paddle steamer "Alexandra", landing on a small pier.

Jabez Spencer Balfour
(1843 - 1916)

A special train decorated with flowers and bunting was waiting to take the party from Bembridge Station (on the opposite side of the road from the Royal Spithead Hotel) to Brading where further guests and a military band were waiting to join the special train. The train returned to Bembridge for lunch to celebrate the occasion.

From the opening, the line was worked under contract by the Isle of Wight Railway for half the receipts but, as they had to supply rolling stock, fuel and crew, it is doubtful whether they made much profit.

In August 1885, the Isle of Wight Marine Transit Company (also part of the Liberator Building Society Group) started a train-ferry steamer service using the former North British Railway's Granton-Burntisland vessel "Carrier", sailing between St. Helens and Langston Harbour on the Hayling Island branch. Unfortunately, the service failed to prosper even though the London, Brighton & South Coast Railway made an agreement with the Isle of Wight Marine Transit Company in December 1885 for the hire of "Carrier" and the use of the quays at St. Helens and Langston. The service discontinued in March 1888.

After experiencing difficult times, Jabez Spencer Balfour and the directors of the Liberator Building Society resorted to using rather dubious methods of maintaining profits but, in September 1892 the crash came when their banking concern suspended payments.

Manning Wardle 0-6-0 saddle tank "Bembridge" at Bembridge Station soon after the station was opened. At this time, the canopy had not been added to the station building. William Weeks, the first Bembridge stationmaster is seen standing on the extreme right of the photograph.

While two of Balfour's associates were arrested in December 1892, Balfour fled the country and took refuge in the Argentine until his whereabouts became known in April 1893. He was arrested in January 1894 but was not finally handed over into British custody until April 1895.

Balfour was to serve most of his prison sentence in, of all places Parkhurst Prison on the Isle of Wight where he was both librarian and organist. He was described as a model prisoner and was released with full remission for good conduct on April 14th, 1906.

The United Realisation Company was formed in May 1895 to take over the assets of the Liberator Building Society and some of its associated companies which included involvement with the Brading Harbour Improvement & Railway Company.

In November 1895, the Brading Harbour Improvement & Railway Company sought and obtained further powers which defined the harbour limits and permitted extensive dredging. At the same time they dropped the word "Improvement" from their title to become the Brading Harbour & Railway Company.

The company engineers were now P. W. Meik and A. C. Schonberg. Not a great deal is known about these two gentlemen apart from the fact that P. W. Meik had been one of the engineers for the construction of the Lee-on-Solent Railway.

A view from the beach of the Royal Spithead Hotel, which was officially opened in 1882 and was also built by the Brading Harbour Improvement & Railway Company as part of their grand plans for the future. Author's Collection

A similar view to page 7 but taken from further back showing the Royal Spithead Hotel (right). Author's Collection

The junction station at Brading with Isle of Wight Railway 2-4-0T "Shanklin" at the branch platform (left) with the Bembridge train, while Isle of Wight Railway 2-4-0T "Brading" (right) leaves for Ryde Pier Head in 1910. Author's Collection

In 1898, the Brading Harbour & Railway Company's undertaking was purchased by the Isle of Wight Railway (who had, of course, operated the line from the outset) for £16,500. The Royal Spithead Hotel had already been sold by the company in 1894.

The Isle of Wight Railway tried a scheme to get passengers to travel to Ventnor by boat from Portsmouth to the small pier at Bembridge (near to the station) and then direct to Ventnor by train. Unfortunately, like the train-ferry service, this scheme was also short lived.

After the 1923 grouping, all the Island's railways passed into the hands of the Southern Railway who in 1928 rebuilt the Medina Wharf in the north of the Island which meant a gradual decline in traffic at St. Helens Quay.

During the Second World War, the line managed to escape with just one or two 'minor incidents', while in 1948, when nationalization took place, the Southern Railway became British Railways Southern Region but, by the early 1950's only the Ryde to Ventnor service remained profitable while the rest of the Island's railways were feeling the effect of motor transport.

The Bembridge branch line finally closed on and from September 21st, 1953. The grand plans laid by Jabez Spencer Balfour and the Brading Harbour Improvement & Railway Company in 1874 were now well and truly over.

After his release from prison in 1906, Jabez Spencer Balfour returned to business as a consulting engineer with an office in Chancery Lane in London. On February 23rd, 1916 at the age of 73 he was travelling to Swansea to take up an appointment with the Morriston Colliery when he suffered a heart attack and was dead when taken from the train at Newport (Monmouthshire, now Gwent).

An unidentified O2 class 0-4-4T waits with the branch train at Bembridge Station in the late 1940's.   W.A.Camwell

Manning Wardle 0-6-0 saddle tank "Bembridge" at Ryde Works in 1892.   Author's Collection

Description of the Route

The Bembridge branch line commenced from a 211 ft long bay at the back of the down platform at Brading Station and faced north towards Ryde. From Brading the single line slightly veered to the left for a short distance running parallel with the main line to Ryde before curving off to the right at a 16 chain radius towards St. Helens and Bembridge.

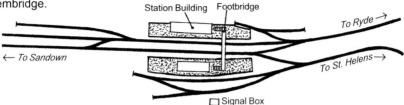

BRADING STATION

O2 class 0-4-4T No.W.20 "Shanklin" with the branch train at Brading Station. September 9th 1937.

S. W. Baker

Having just left Brading with the Bembridge train, O2 class 0-4-4T No.W.14 "Fishbourne" curves away from the main line. September 7th 1952. D. Trevor Rowe

After 34 chains, the line reached the level crossing and sidings at Brading Quay which formed the original branch before the line was extended to Bembridge. Because the crossing and sidings at one time served some cement mills, the crossing became locally known as Cement Mills Crossing. The sidings, which were controlled from a small ground level signal box were also used for storing redundant rolling stock.

The ground level signal box at the Cement Mills Crossing, Brading Quay in the early 1950's. Note the "Shooting, Fishing and Egging Prohibited" notice.   Author's Collection

Seventy chains further on, a siding known as Carpenters was passed on the left of the line. This siding was described as the Brickfield Siding when Col. Yolland inspected the line for the Board of Trade prior to the opening for passengers. The siding was removed in 1946 and two gates were placed there as a cattle crossing to enable the farmer, a Mr. Lovegrove, to put his cattle in the fields on the other side of the line.

From here the line slowly curved to the right before it reached St. Helens Station with its single 232 ft long platform which was on the down side of the line and was 1 mile 55 chains from Brading. The station building, which was similar to the one at Bembridge, was (and still is) a most impressive brick building with dormer windows but, unlike Bembridge the less interesting side of the building faced the railway while the imposing side faced the hill towards St. Helens village.

The station layout was completed with a signal box for working in and out of the sidings on St. Helens Quay although the signal box was later withdrawn by the Southern Railway in favour of a ground frame.

St. Helens Quay was reached by passing over the embankment toll road by a level crossing and consisted of sidings on the north and south quay. The quayside boasted a weighbridge, a large goods shed, a small engine shed and at one time as many as four cranes, one of which was hand operated while the others were mobile steam cranes. The small engine shed was built to house the Manning Wardle 0-6-0 saddle tank "Bembridge" when the branch first opened but, after 1921 this building ceased to be an engine shed and was later used by the Permanent Way Department.

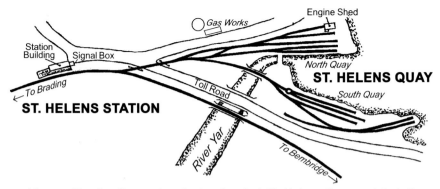

Messrs Chaplins the carriers had a depot at St. Helens Quay and their three boats, the *Wild Swan*, the *Excelsior* and the *Asteroid* unloaded merchandise on the quay where it was loaded into covered goods wagons and later taken to Ryde St. Johns Road. Messrs Longs and Messrs Curtess also had berths at the quay.

As mentioned in the history of the line, St. Helens Quay was used for a train-ferry steamer service from Langston Harbour on the Hayling Island branch and, although this service failed after three years, St. Helens was still a very busy port for many years.

At one time, a 1ft 11½ins narrow gauge railway connected the nearby St. Helens Gas Works with the quayside and was used for conveying coal and coke in small tipper wagons.

St. Helens Station on February 5th 1952.　　　　　　　John H. Meredith

12

Terrier 0-6-0T No.W.13 "Carisbrooke" propels push-and-pull set No.484 to Bembridge having just left St. Helens Station on April 11th 1936. S.W.Baker

(*Above left*) The approach to St. Helens Quay in 1920 with the small weighbridge hut on the left of the photograph. (*Above right*) Messrs Chaplins boat the *Excelsior* at the north quay. Author's Collection

St. Helens Quay from the south side. St Helens Station can just be seen in the top left-hand corner.
A.B.MacLeod/WLS Collection

On leaving St. Helens, the line curved to the right towards Bembridge and ran parallel to the toll road, first crossing the River Yar by a steel bridge and then continuing across an area known as Bembridge Lagoon following a curve to the left followed by a bend to the right before entering Bembridge Station which was 2 miles 61 chains from Brading, on a 1 in 600 rising gradient.

As previously mentioned, the station building was very similar to that at St. Helens but, here the impressive side of the building was on the 220 ft long platform facing the railway.

On the approach to the station was a short siding to the left which was known as the coal siding and had covered coal staithes. The station layout was completed with a signal box which was situated on the platform next to the station building, a turntable and a run round loop plus a siding which was alongside the loop and was also used by coal merchants and general freight trains.

The 25ft diameter turntable which was installed in April 1936 replaced the original even smaller turntable which was a mere 16ft 5ins. Locomotives were only partly turned on the turntable to get on to the run round loop, instead of the more usual arrangement of a shunting neck and points for access to the run round loop. This unusual arrangement was due to the lack of space.

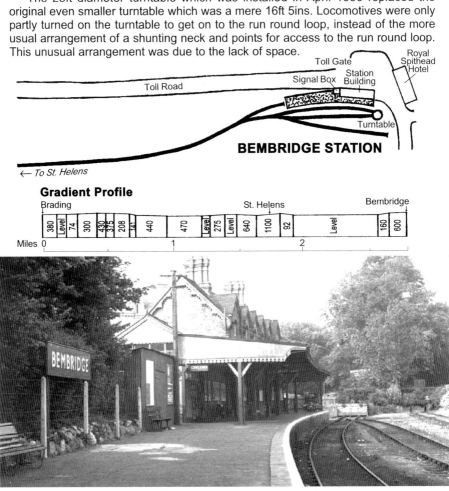

Bembridge Station on July 4th 1953.   R.F.Roberts

14

View of Bembridge Station from the other side of the turntable.

Replacing the small turntable by one of 25ft diameter at Bembridge Station. April 11th 1936.

Motive Power and Rolling Stock

As mentioned in the history of the line, "Bembridge" the Manning Wardle 0-6-0 saddle tank was used by the contactors Scott & Edwards in the construction of the branch and when their work was completed in March 1882, this small locomotive was sold for £650 to the Brading Harbour Improvement & Railway Company.

"Bembridge" was to work the branch from the opening right up until 1916 (having passed into the ownership of the Isle of Wight Railway for £430 in 1898) when it was sold to the War Dept., and left the Island to be employed on the Fovant Military Railway in Wiltshire and later went abroad.

Manning Wardle 0-6-0 saddle tank "Bembridge" on the turntable at Bembridge Station. Note how the original capped chimney (see pages 7 and 9) had been replaced by a rather plain looking stove pipe design.   M. Lawson Finch Collection

"St. Helens" the 2-4-0 well tank which was the other locomotive used by Scott & Edwards during construction, was also obtained by the Brading Harbour Improvement & Railway Company but was only steamed when "Bembridge" was receiving routine maintenance. In September 1893, "St. Helens" was sold to Charles Westwood the contractor of the Newport, Godshill & St. Lawrence Railway for £650 where as "St. Lawrence," it was employed in that line's construction.

In April 1905, Dugald Drummond, the London & South Western Railway Locomotive Superintendent was commissioned at a fee of £150 to visit the Bembridge branch and estimate the cost of operating a Steam Railcar, similar to the type that Drummond had provided for several branch lines on the London & South Western Railway. Although savings would have been possible, they were considered insufficient to warrant the purchase of a Steam Railcar from Beyer Peacock & Co.

When "Bembridge" was sold to the War Dept., in 1916, the branch locomotive's duties were shared by one of the Isle of Wight Railway's 2-4-0T's which they had obtained from Beyer Peacock & Co. Of these locomotives, "Ryde", "Sandown" and "Shanklin" arrived in 1864, "Ventnor" in 1868, "Brading" in 1876 and "Bonchurch" in 1883. With the exception of "Bonchurch" which, because of its larger bunker was unable to use the turntable at Bembridge, all these locomotives saw service on the branch.

On its way to the Island by boat in 1883, "Bonchurch" made a big splash when it fell into the sea as it approached St. Helens Quay. It stayed there for a day or two before finally being dragged to the quayside, none too worse for its adventure.

Isle of Wight Railway 2-4-0T "Ryde" at Bembridge Station.   C. Woodnutt/WLS Collection

Isle of Wight Railway 2-4-0T "Ventnor" having just left St. Helens with the branch train for Bembridge. June 15th 1923.   H. C. Casserley

After the Southern Railway absorbed all the Island's railways at the time of the 1923 grouping, three of the former London, Brighton & South Coast Railway "Terrier" 0-6-0T's (designed by William Stroudley) which had been working on the Isle of Wight Central Railway, saw service on the branch and were soon joined by three more "Terriers" which the Southern Railway obtained from their mainland stock. Also, two former Isle of Wight Central Railway Beyer Peacock 2-4-0T's Nos. 5 & 8, which were slightly smaller than the previously mentioned Isle of Wight Railway Beyer Peacock locomotives, saw out their days on the branch.

In May 1923, when the first two former London & South Western Railway O2 class 0-4-4T's, designed by William Adams, arrived on the Island, they worked the Ryde to Ventnor trains with great success and burnt less fuel than the former Isle of Wight Railway Beyer Peacock 2-4-0T's. By 1936 there were twenty O2's working on the Island's railways so it was decided to strengthen the track to Bembridge and enlarge the small turntable so that the O2's could also be used on the branch. From this time onwards, the O2's predominated the work until the branch closed.

O2 class 0-4-4T No.W.20 "Shanklin" on the new turntable at Bembridge Station. September 9th 1937.   S.W.Baker

Terrier 0-6-0T No.W.9 "Fishbourne" at Bembridge Station with the branch train.   Lens of Sutton

The former Isle of Wight Central Railway 2-4-0T No.8 built by Beyer Peacock and seen here at Bembridge Station as Southern Railway No.W.8. Lens of Sutton

O2 class 0-4-4T No.W.14 "Fishbourne" approaching St. Helens from Bembridge in 1948. E.C.Griffiths

As part of the agreement for working the line, the Isle of Wight Railway supplied all the rolling stock so, when opened for passengers in 1882, they would probably have used 4-wheel carriages which the Isle of Wight Railway had bought new between 1864 and 1866.

It was generally thought that when horse trams were no longer required on Ryde Pier, two of the carriages were bought by the Isle of Wight Railway in 1886 for use on the Bembridge branch although, more recent research has thrown doubt on this. What might have caused this confusion over the years was probably the three carriages which were obtained from the Oldbury Wagon Company (full company name 'Railway Carriage Company Limited of Oldbury', near Birmingham). These carriages were originally supplied to the Golden Valley Railway in 1881 but, due to lack of funds, were returned to the Oldbury Wagon Company. Two of the carriages were 6-wheel saloons, one first class and the other second class with open balconies at each end displaying decorative ironwork bearing the intials 'G.V.' The third carriage was a guard's van with a balcony, side doors and lookouts. These three carriages worked on the branch for many years and were eventually replaced by former North London Railway 4-wheel stock which had been obtained in 1897 and 1898.

From 1924, former London, Brighton & South Coast Railway 4-wheelers were used followed by odd loose stock which included the carriage portion of the former Isle of Wight Central Railway Steam Railcar No.1 plus a former Great Eastern Railway 4-wheel carriage.

In April 1925, four former South Eastern & Chatham Railway Steam Railcar carriages which had been converted to pairs of open bogie carriages were transferred to the Island for intended push-and-pull duties but due to a shortage of push-and-pull stock on the Southern system, were returned to the mainland in 1927 although before leaving, they did make a brief appearance on the Bembridge branch where they were locomotive hauled rather than push-and-pull.

While the turntable at Bembridge was being enlarged in 1936, the branch did see push-and-pull service in the shape of two former London, Chatham & Dover Railway 4-wheel carriages forming set No. 484 and were pulled by Stroudley "Terrier" No. W.13 "Carisbrooke". With set No. 483 also fitted for push-and-pull service and mainly used on the Ventnor West branch, these former London, Chatham & Dover Railway carriages were originally built as 6-wheelers.

From 1938 onwards former London, Brighton & South Coast Railway push-and-pull stock arrived for duties on the branch where they were always locomotive hauled and sometimes ran with an additional carriage.

The three former Golden Valley Railway carriages at Bembridge Station.   Author's Collection

Push-and-pull set No.484 arriving at Bembridge while being propelled by "Terrier" 0-6-0T
No.W.13 "Carisbrooke" in 1936.
Lens of Sutton

Former Isle of Wight Central Railway 2-4-0T No.W.5 at Bembridge Station in 1925 with the
former South Eastern & Chatham Steam Railcar coaches which had been converted to pairs
of open bogie carriages.
Bluebell R.P.S. Archives

Operation

When the line first opened, the branch engine was stabled overnight in the small shed on St. Helens Quay, but, by 1921 the daily engine to work the branch would leave the locomotive shed at Ryde St. Johns Road at 5.00am and remain on the branch till the service finished around 10.30pm or 11 pm. This involved three sets of engine crews, i.e. early, middle and late.

On weekdays, the coaching stock was left at Bembridge but, on Saturdays after the last passenger service to Bembridge was completed, the train was run empty to Brading ready for Sunday working.

The water for the branch engine was contained in two large tanks at the southern end of Brading Station. In later years, the water was pumped up by a pipe leading from the River Yar using a two stroke Petters engine. The employees who started this engine were paid 2/6d (12$\frac{1}{2}$p) a week extra to their wages.

There were two breaks of service during the day, one at 10.30am approximately to enable a goods train to take permanent way materials from St. Helens to Sandown for various parts of the Island railway system. This could be anything from rail sleepers or ballast to empty tar tanks for Shanklin Gas Works. Then a break in the early afternoon for cleaning the engine.

Although the branch was worked by the 'one engine in steam' principle from when it first opened, it was still considered necessary in those days to provide signalling.

Signal boxes were provided at Brading, Cement Mills Crossing at Brading Quay, St. Helens and at Bembridge.

The Southern Railway virtually abolished all the signalling on the line when it became accepted practice to work 'one engine in steam' lines without signals. The signal box at St. Helens was also withdrawn and the connection to the Quay was worked from a ground frame.

O2 class 0-4-4T No.W.14 "Fishbourne" on the turntable at Bembridge Station. September 13th 1952.

F. Hornby

The train staff was shaped like a half moon at one end and a key at the other end and was kept in the signal box at Brading. This staff opened the Annetts locks at the Cement Mills Crossing at Brading Quay, the ground frame at St. Helens for entrance to the Quay and the signal box at Bembridge. It would have also been used at Carpenters Siding before the siding was lifted although during the Isle of Wight Railway days, when the small engine shed was in use on St. Helens Quay, the Annetts key for Carpenters Siding was kept at St. Helens Station.

Terrier 0-6-0T No.W.13 "Carisbrooke" in the branch bay at Brading Station.   Lens of Sutton

O2 class 0-4-4T No.W.14 "Fishbourne" with branch train at Bembridge Station. May 23rd 1953.

R. F. Roberts

Life on the "Bembridge Branch"

From its earliest days, the branch became affectionately known as "The Crabby Winkle Line" due to the fact that its original engine was the small Manning Wardle 0-6-0 saddle tank "Bembridge" and this name was handed down by the locals through the years right up to the closure.

The boys from Bembridge School on the outskirts of Bembridge always used the branch to travel to and from Bembridge during their holidays at Easter, Summer and Christmas.

During the month of August, the branch was very busy on Sundays with the Boys' Brigade, Church Lads' Brigade and Girl Guides who camped at St. Helens and at Bembridge. The Crusaders Union Boys also came at this time, but they stayed at Bembridge School.

The first stationmaster at Bembridge was William Weeks who was appointed at the age of 24, having previously been in charge of the small station at Wroxall. William Weeks, who lived in the stationmaster's house at Bembridge, was from a railway family and three of his brothers also became stationmasters at Chester, Rhyl and Sheffield respectively, while another brother became a toll gate keeper at Bembridge on returning from the Boer War. Also, two of William Weeks' sons were later employed by the Isle of Wight Railway and one of these, Tom Weeks became stationmaster at St. Helens where he also had charge of St. Helens Quay.

Unfortunately, William Weeks died at the early age of 33 and his family had to move from the stationmaster's house and went to live nearby at Harbour Garden Cottage.

When a Ladies' Golf Club was opened on part of the reclaimed land, Mrs. Weeks became the Club's Stewardess for a number of years.

Manning Wardle 0-6-0 saddle tank "Bembridge" at Bembridge Station in 1911.   Lens of Sutton

One interesting story that Mrs. Weeks passed on to her grandaughter Mrs. Violet Dyer (Tom Weeks' daughter) was that when the rails were laid at Bembridge Station, they should have been put on the other side of the building (like St. Helens) but, the company found that there would not be room for any other outside traffic between the station and the sea if they did. They built the line so far and then stopped just short of the building where it was used as a coal depot for a local coal man and so did not interfere with outside traffic.

This is an interesting theory as both St. Helens and Bembridge Stations were built in 1877, five years before the line was completed and could explain why one faced the platform and one faced the other way.

One person whose knowledge of the Bembridge branch was of great help to the author, was Roy Way, who started work for the Isle of Wight Railway at Ryde St. Johns Road in February 1924 and, after a spell as grade 1 porter/signalman at Newchurch Station on the Newport to Sandown line, moved to Brading Station as porter/signalman in 1941 and remained there until November 1974 when he retired after 50 years 9 months on the Island's railways.

Two passenger guards who mainly worked early and late shifts on the branch during Roy Way's time at Brading were Walter Buckett and Alfred Dallimore while the Brading stationmaster Mr. H. Attril and his successor Mr. Stan Martin used to make out the shunters list for the branch goods train to shunt the sidings at St. Helens Quay before going on to Bembridge.

At this time, the Cement Mills Crossing at Brading Quay was operated by a Mrs. Deacon, who lived in the crossing keeper's cottage with her husband who was also employed on the railway as a member of the Brading Permanent Way Gang which looked after track maintenance. When Mrs. Deacon had her annual holiday, her duties were usually handled by the staff at Brading Station.

The staff at Bembridge Station during these later days of the branch, consisted of Walter Lee who was booking clerk and lived in the stationmaster's house and Charlie Wetherick who was grade 1 porter and lived at St. Helens in the village. These two gentlemen shared early and late turns alternatively.

O2 class 0-4-4T No. W.20 "Shanklin" on the turntable at Bembridge Station in the 1940's. Lens of Sutton

Timetables

1884

WEEK DAYS / SUNDAYS

	a.m	a.m	p.m	p.m	p.m	p.m	p.m	p.m	p.m	p.m	p.m
									SUNDAYS		
Brading Junction	8.37	10.52	1.41	3.40	5.51	8.16	1.03	2.10	3.10	4.37	8.57
St. Helens	8.42	10.57	1.46	3.45	5.56	8.21	1.08	2.15	3.15	4.42	9.02
Bembridge	8.47	11.02	1.51	3.50	6.01	8.26	1.13	2.20	3.20	4.47	9.07

WEEK DAYS / SUNDAYS

	a.m	a.m	p.m	p.m	p.m	p.m	p.m	p.m	p.m	p.m	p.m
									SUNDAYS		
Bembridge	8.13	10.35	1.12	3.20	5.35	7.48	12.47	1.55	2.55	4.20	7.37
St. Helens	8.17	10.40	1.17	3.25	5.40	7.53	12.52	2.00	3.00	4.25	7.42
Brading Junction	8.21	10.45	1.22	3.30	5.45	7.58	12.57	2.05	3.04	4.30	7.47

1922

WEEK DAYS

	a.m	a.m	a.m	p.m	p.m	p.m	p.m	p.m	p.m	p.m
Brading Junction	8.18	A9.40	10.47	12.46	1.50	2.35	3.10	4.35	5.02	6.03
St. Helens	8.23	A9.45	10.52	12.51	1.55	2.40	3.15	4.40	5.07	6.08
Bembridge	8.28	A9.50	10.57	12.56	2.00	2.45	3.20	4.45	5.12	6.13

WEEK DAYS CONT. / SUNDAYS

	p.m	p.m	p.m	p.m	p.m	p.m	p.m	p.m
Brading Junction	7.26	9.40	2.39	3.25	4.37	6.05	8.03	9.05
St. Helens	7.31	9.45	2.44	3.30	4.42	6.10	8.08	9.10
Bembridge	7.36	9.50	2.49	3.35	4.47	6.15	8.13	9.15

A Mondays only.

WEEK DAYS

	a.m	a.m	a.m	p.m	p.m	p.m	p.m	p.m	p.m
Bembridge	8.00	A9.25	10.30	12.08	1.23	2.17	2.55	4.00	5.45
St. Helens	8.05	A9.30	10.35	12.13	1.28	2.22	3.00	4.05	5.50
Brading Junction	8.10	A9.35	10.40	12.18	1.33	2.27	3.05	4.10	5.55

WEEK DAYS CONT. / SUNDAYS

	p.m	p.m	p.m	p.m	p.m	p.m	p.m	p.m
Bembridge	7.00	8.50	2.23	3.10	4.17	5.50	7.50	8.48
St. Helens	7.05	8.55	2.28	3.15	4.22	5.55	7.55	8.53
Brading Junction	7.10	9.00	2.33	3.20	4.27	6.00	8.00	8.58

A Mondays only.

Aerial view of Bembridge Station with the Royal Spithead Hotel on the left of the photograph in 1938.

A Selection of Tickets

Isle of Wight Ry.
ST. HELENS
Series 1 TO
BEMBRIDGE
THIRD CLASS FARE 1½d
Not Transferable. Issued subject to the
Co's Bye Laws & Published Regulations

JU 29 06 6490

Isle of Wight Ry.
Available day of issue only.
BEMBRIDGE
Series 6) TO
BRADING
THIRD CLASS FARE 4½d
Not Transferable. Issued subject to the
Co's Bye Laws & Published Regulations

2320 2320

SOUTHERN RAILWAY.
This ticket is issued subject to the Company's
Bye-laws, Regulations and Conditions in their
Time Tables, Notices and Book of Regulations.
Available on DAY of issue ONLY.
Bembridge to
Bembridge   Bembridge
Ryde Esp.   Ryde Esp.
RYDE ESPLANADE
Via Brading
Third Class   Third Class
Fare 11½d   Fare 11½d

2127 2127

BRITISH RAILWAYS (S)
This ticket is issued subject to the Bye-laws,
Regulations and Conditions contained in the
Publications and Notices of and applicable to the
Railway Executive.
Brading to
Brading   Brading
St.Helens   St.Helens
ST. HELENS
THIRD CLASS   THIRD CLASS
Fare 4d,H   Fare 4d H
NOT TRANSFERABLE.

7499 7499

Tickets from the G.R.Croughton Collection.

SOUTHERN RAILWAY.
BRADING HARBOUR EMBANKMENT
ROAD & WORKS
2D
Receipt for one of the
Twopenny Tolls
enumerated in the author-
ised List exhibited upon the
Bridge premises.
FOR CONDITIONS SEE BACK

D 2158

(Above left) William Cranwell issues tickets for the toll road between Bembridge and St. Helens which was owned by the railway. Southern Railway Magazine. *(Above right)* A toll ticket. G.R.Croughton Collection

O2 class 0-4-4T No.W.14 "Fishbourne" at Brading Station with the branch train on September 7th 1952.

D. Trevor Rowe

Closure

One of the rather sad facts of progress in the immediate years after World War II was that many branch lines and light railways were beginning to feel the effect of motor transport which resulted in less rail travel, especially during the winter months.

The early 1950's brought closures to several similar lines which were running at a loss and, unfortunately for the Isle of Wight and rural railway enthusiasts alike, British Railways Southern Region announced that the Merstone to Ventnor West line would close on and from September 15th, 1952. The following year they announced that not only the Bembridge branch would close on and from September 21st, 1953, but also the Freshwater, Yarmouth & Newport line plus the stations at Wootton and Whippingham on the Ryde to Newport line.

Opposition by local people to keep these services came to nothing - it very rarely did.

The last day's service was on September 20th, 1953 and, as the locomotive which normally worked the branch at the time, Adams O2 class 0-4-4T No. W.14 "Fishbourne" was unavailable, the final train was pulled by O2 class No. W.28 "Ashey".

For the very last run from Brading, every seat seemed to be occupied by local people and railway enthusiasts making a last sentimental journey across the reclaimed marsh to Bembridge. One such person was Herbert Occomore, a former Harbour Master and Pilot at Bembridge who had travelled on the first train from Brading to St. Helens in 1881.

The driver was Jack W. Jeffries, the fireman was Albert Lock and the guard was Fred Jenvey who wore a carnation in his buttonhole specially for the occasion.

On leaving Brading, the train was brought to an abrupt halt when someone pulled the communication cord. No sooner had it restarted when the same thing happened again. This treatment went on for several more times in a distance of about a 100 yards, adding to the fact that detonators had been put on the line, so a few bangs were also heard.

The driver and guard were now getting really fed up with the whole business of getting out of the train and walking the track to find out which carriage was responsible for the incident. In the end, the guard shut off the Westinghouse brake and the train carried on to Bembridge relying on the hand brake and the engine brake.

On arriving at Bembridge, the train was loudly and heartily greeted by a band.

After the engine was turned for the last time on the small turntable and the crowd had dispersed, the train pulled sadly away from Bembridge never to return with a passenger service.

O2 class 0-4-4T No. W.28 "Ashey" approaching St Helens Station on September 20th, 1953, the last day of public service.   Pamlin Prints

The Present Scene

At Brading Station, the bay for Bembridge is still in evidence although the trackbed is now very overgrown.

The signal box, which was built for the opening of the Bembridge branch in 1882 and closed in 1988 is at the time of writing still there but, with the branch tracks long since removed, it now looks rather detached from the rest of the station.

From Brading, the overgrown trackbed curves away to the right from the line to Ryde and soon becomes a public footpath before reaching the site of the Cement Mills Crossing at the former Brading Quay.

At this point it is very hard to imagine that there ever was a crossing or signal box or even a cement mill and even harder to imagine that this was once a quay although there is still a nearby hollow known as "Boat Bottom" where ships used to tie up.

From here the route continues and makes a most enjoyable walk across the reclaimed marsh towards St. Helens.

The former station at St. Helens is now converted into a fine private residence partially hidden by trees, while houses have now been built over the former sidings on St. Helens Quay.

The gas holder which stood near to the level crossing which led to the quay, and was a land mark as far as the branch was concerned, was dismantled during October 1983.

On leaving St. Helens, the abutments which carried the line to Bembridge over the River Yar can still be seen next to the road bridge. The road at this point was, of course, the former toll road which remained a toll road even after the railway closed until it was sold to the County Council in 1971 who then abolished the toll.

The overgrown Bembridge bay at Brading Station on October 28th 1987. Although the signal box was still in use at that time, this view shows how detached it had become from the rest of the station. Author

Although the line closed in 1953, the station building at Bembridge stood in a derelict condition (see page 32) until 1970 when it was finally demolished. On the same spot today stands a small estate of terrace houses giving no indication that this was ever a railway station.

The former railway-owned Royal Spithead Hotel was demolished in 1989 to be replaced by a town house development.

Fortunately, steam trains on the Island in the shape of "O2" class No. W.24 "Calbourne" and "Terriers" 0-6-0T No. W.8 "Freshwater" and No.W.11 "Newport" can still be seen in action thanks to the largely volunteer run Isle of Wight Steam Railway, which began operating trains in 1971 at their Haven Street headquarters. The line now extends five miles from Wootton, through Haven Street and Ashey, to Smallbrook Junction, which is the interchange with the Island Line's electric trains that run from Ryde Pier Head to Shanklin.

Looking towards St. Helens from Brading where the former trackbed now forms a footpath. October 28th 1987.   Author

The abutments of the bridge which carried the line over the River Yar at St. Helens. The former St. Helens Station (now a private house) can just be seen in the trees on the left of the photograph.
Author

30

Conclusion

The grand scheme to reclaim the seabed at Brading Harbour and develop St. Helens and Bembridge never reached the optimistic hopes of the Brading Harbour Improvement & Railway Company. Consequently the Bembridge branch line never really had a chance to become anything more than just a simple country railway.

After the closing of the Cement Mills at Brading Quay and the later decline of St. Helens Quay, the railway was only carrying a few passengers mostly during the summer months and finally closed in September 1953 having supposedly served its purpose.

To watch the small branch train rattling across the reclaimed marsh and then to watch the locomotive partly turned on the small turntable at Bembridge brings the memory back to a time gone by when the world seemed to operate at a more leisurely pace.

The Bembridge branch line will always be associated with this leisurely pace of life.

O2 class 0-4-4T No.W.17 "Seaview" at Bembridge Station.   Lens of Sutton

Terrier 0-6-0T No.W.13 "Carisbrooke" at St. Helens Station with push-and-pull set No.484 on April 11th 1936.   S.W.Baker

Acknowledgements

When I wrote the first edition of this publication in 1988, I appealled for information in the *Isle of Wight County Press* and was very grateful for the help I received from Roy Way who so willingly compiled many interesting notes on the line which were backed up by his 50 years experience on the Island's railways (many of which were in the Brading Signal Box). Also from that same appeal I received most interesting letters from Mrs V. Dyer and Mrs M.R.Sears who both passed on their fond memories from days gone by at Bembridge and St. Helens.

Many thanks also to the following people and organisations for their kind help in compiling information and supplying photographs for both the original and revised publication. John Scott-Morgan and members of the Wight Locomotive Society, Godfrey Croughton, John H. Meredith, D. Trevor Rowe, Alan A. Jackson, Frank Hornby, Nick Catford, Pamlin Prints, Bluebell R.P.S. Archives, Isle of Wight County Press and the Isle of Wight County Records Office.

I would also like to place on record the help with photograhs that I have received over the years from the following gentleman who are unfortunately no longer with us:- Mr.S.W.Baker, Mr.R.F.Roberts, Mr.M.Lawson Finch, Mr.J.L.Smith, Mr.H.C.Casserley and Mr.W.A.Camwell.

My thanks as always to Norman Branch for kindly reading my text and to James Christian of Binfield Printers Ltd.

Bibliography

THE ISLE OF WIGHT RAILWAY by R. J. Maycock and R. Silsbury (Oakwood Press)
THE ISLE OF WIGHT RAILWAYS by Michael Robbins (Oakwood Press)
A LOCOMOTIVE HISTORY OF RAILWAYS ON THE ISLE OF WIGHT by D. L. Bradley (The Railway Correspondence and Travel Society)
SOUTHERN RAILWAY BRANCH LINE TRAINS by R. W. Kidner (Oakwood Press)
RAILS IN THE ISLE OF WIGHT by P. C. Allen and A. B. MacLeod (David & Charles)
ONCE UPON A LINE Vol. 1 & 2 by Andrew Britton (Oxford Publishing)
ISLE OF WIGHT RAILWAYS REMEMBERED by Peter Paye (Oxford Publishing)
RYDE TO VENTNOR by Vic Mitchell and Keith Smith (Middleton Press)
WIGHT REPORT (Various issues)
RAILWAY MAGAZINE (Various issues)
RAILWAY WORLD (Various issues)

The derelict Bembridge Station in October 1967.   Nick Catford